For the students of St. Elizabeth School —B.H.

Library of Congress Cataloging-in-Publication Data
Names: Heos, Bridget, author. | Clark, David, illustrator.
Title: Just like us!, crocs / by Bridget Heos ; illustrated by David Clark.
Other titles: Crocs
Description: Boston : Houghton Mifflin Harcourt, [2019] | Series: Just like us! | Audience:
Age 4–7. | Audience: K to Grade 3. | Includes bibliographical references.
Identifiers: LCCN 2018034455 | ISBN 9781328791924 (paper over board) |
ISBN 9780358003908 (paperback) | ISBN 9780358055846 (ebook)
Subjects: LCSH: Crocodilians—Juvenile literature. |
Crocodilians—Behavior—Juvenile literature.
Classification: LCC QL666.C9 H46 2019 | DDC 597.98—dc23
LC record available at https://lccn.loc.gov/2018034455

Manufactured in China
SCP 10 9 8 7 6 5 4 3 2 1
4500755773

Lexile Level	Guided Reading	Fountas & Pinnell	Interest Level
NC830L	Q	Q	Grade 2–6

JUST LIKE US! CROCS

by Bridget Heos

illustrated by David Clark

HOUGHTON MIFFLIN HARCOURT

Boston   New York

CROCS

The Inside Scoop

ALLIGATORS AND CROCODILES have large mouths, short legs, and powerful tails. Humans have small mouths, long legs, and no tails at all. But crocodilians (which include alligators, crocodiles, muggers, caimans, and gharials) *are* like us in some ways. They love to bask in the sun and cool off with a swim. Unlike most reptiles, crocs are quite social. They live in groups and are attentive parents. Read on to learn all about our congenial crocodilian comrades!

HOLE SWEET HOLE

PEOPLE BUILD SHELTERS to survive harsh conditions. Crocs construct homes of sorts too. American alligators living in the swamps and marshes of the Florida Everglades have an endless supply of water during the warmer months, when it storms daily. But as the temperature cools, the rains stop and the swamps dry up. So alligators take matters into their own claws, digging holes that remain full of water throughout the year. The holes provide a home not just for the alligators, but also for other fresh-water animals. Everybody wins! (Except for those animals eaten by their bigger and stronger hole-mates.)

Team(*gulp*)work! In places like Mexico and Central and South America, crocodilians survive the dry season by crowding into the remaining wetlands. Just as humans have historically teamed up to hunt for food, so does the common caiman. At night, groups of caimans have been observed fanning out beneath water cascading from a higher part of the pond. With open mouths, they await a school of fish traveling downstream. For the fish, there is no escape—the caimans' mouths act as one giant trap. Chomp!

OH, BELLOW THERE!

CROCODILIANS COMMUNICATE in many ways. American alligators introduce themselves by bellowing. Through this noisy growl, the alligator tells the others a little about itself—whether it's male or female, how big it is, and its location. Another common gesture is the head slap. A croc opens its mouth and then clamps it shut on the water's surface, making a terrific clapping sound. If one croc slaps its head, they all do. Even those underwater will surface to join in the fun. However, just as a smile among humans can mean many things—from friendliness to mischievousness—so can the head slap. Dominant males head-slap to show who's in charge! Ha, ha! That's a head-slapper, boss!

SAY IT WITH BUBBLES!

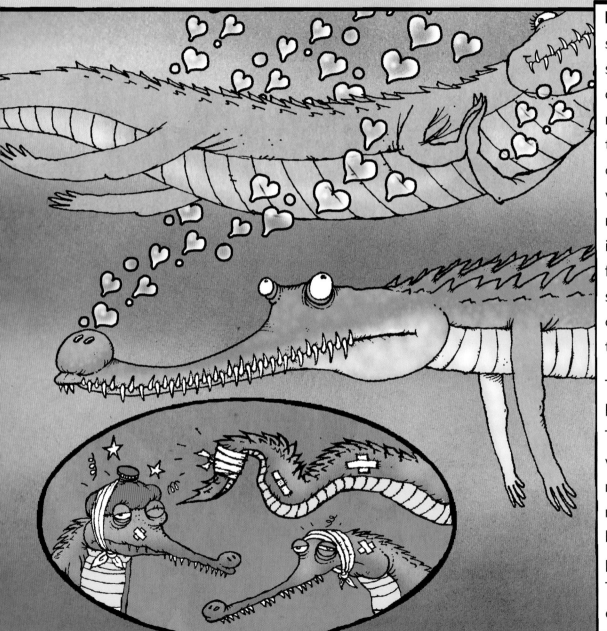

EACH YEAR, LOVE FILLS the air like swamp gas. But not every croc gets a sweetheart. The biggest males chase off the smaller—and usually younger—males, biting their tails as they flee. Then the big daddies engage in head-to-head combat . . . literally. Two dominant males will head-butt each other until one retreats in defeat. Then the victor settles in for a romantic evening. He and a female circle around each other and rub snouts. Next, in an act of pure poetry, one dives down and blows bubbles on the other's belly.

The male gharial has a special growth on his nose that helps with blowing bubbles. This *ghara* looks like a little round pot with nostrils, and indeed that's the meaning of the word in Hindi (minus the nostrils). Swoon! Females are attracted by the lovely buzzing sound the *ghara* produces and the bubbles it makes. The pair mates, and soon the female is expecting eggs.

Crush Your Vitamins! A pregnant crocodilian needs proper nutrition. In particular, her eggs need calcium to grow strong. Crocodilians don't drink milk. Instead, the mother ingests her calcium from the bones of the animals she eats! In the case of gharials, that's fish. *Bone* appétit! Crunch, crunch!

NO NESTPASSING!

SOME CROCODILIANS BUILD their nests with leaves and grass. Others, such as muggers, dig holes. Mama Mugger digs several before settling into the perfect spot. Then she lays her eggs. Crocodilians are unique in the animal world. Most animals have either large litters that they leave to fend for themselves or small litters that they protect. Crocodilians have large litters, but they protect them carefully. Mama Mugger lays twenty-five to thirty eggs at a time, covering them with mud and then guarding them. Of course, she can't sit on the nest like a bird—she'd crush the eggs! Instead, she digs a muddy hole beside the nest and wallows there. If a thieving snake or lizard comes close, she chases it off, or simply eats it. Mmm, what a tasty intruder!

BEWARE!

The Cool Kids. Whether hatchlings become males or females depends on the temperature inside the nest. In cooler nests, females develop, and in warmer nests, males develop. The Schneider's dwarf caiman lives in the rainforests of South America. With little sunlight streaming in, the nest isn't warm enough for the eggs to develop into males or females. So the caimans use an incubator of sorts. They build their nests beside termite nests. The heat from the termite chamber warms the eggs so both sexes can develop.

BABIES ON BOARD!

MOTHER CROCODILIANS DO most of the parenting. But in some species, fathers pitch in. Muggers are one example of claws-on fathers. While they do not mate for life, they often reside in the same territory as the mother and share in their hatchlings' care. When the baby crocs are ready to hatch, they squeak noisily. They could peck their way out of the shells on their own. But Mom and Dad are happy to help. (They're just wee babies, after all!) The mugger parents dig out the eggs and then roll them around in their mouths, gently cracking them with their teeth. Once the babies are out of the shells, the muggers carry their young to the water in their mouths.

Many a snake or fish would eat the hatchlings in a single bite. But in the shallows of the swamp, mugger families stick together. The hatchlings gather to form a group called a pod. During the day, they sunbathe—often on Mom's or Dad's back. At night, they hunt, though clumsily. They make a squeaking noise when they see something new. They also squeak to let one another know where they are. And they squeak when they're in danger. Then Mama, Daddy, and any other grownups in the area come running. You mess with one mugger, you mess with all muggers!

Baby Food. A baby crocodile has a big snack while still inside the egg: the yolk! Inside the shell, the yolk is nestled next to the developing crocodile. Tiny vessels carry nutrients from the yolk to the inside of the little croc's belly. It's enough to keep it full for up to four months after hatching! Then the crocodile hunts. Of course, a baby can't bring down a zebra or wildebeest. It starts small, chomping down on a cricket or frog, or leaping out of the water to catch a dragonfly. Buzz, buzz, snap!

WELCOME TO THE FAMILY!

WHEN DROUGHT STRIKES, caimans crowd into the remaining swamps. Like people in a crowded place, they mostly tolerate one another. Unlike people, the adult caimans eat any hatchling that wanders their way. The reason is simple: the grownups are hungry. To keep her babies safe, Mama Caiman must find a new swamp. They set out during the cool of night. By the time the sun rises, the heat could be deadly for the out-of-water caimans. Sometimes, the hurried mother finds a swamp where another family is already living. In that case, she can't stay, because she would be seen as a threat. But her harmless babies can. And so she leaves them there, and they become part of a new family.

Smile, Smile, Crocodile. Humans have baby teeth and adult teeth. So do crocodiles. They just have more sets of them! By the time a crocodile is 12.8 feet (3.9 meters) long, it has had forty-five sets of teeth! Teeth are a good way to tell alligators and crocodiles apart. Crocodiles' bottom teeth are visible when their mouths are closed. Alligators' bottom teeth are hidden. Alligators also have wider snouts.

STOP EATING YOUR BROTHERS AND SISTERS

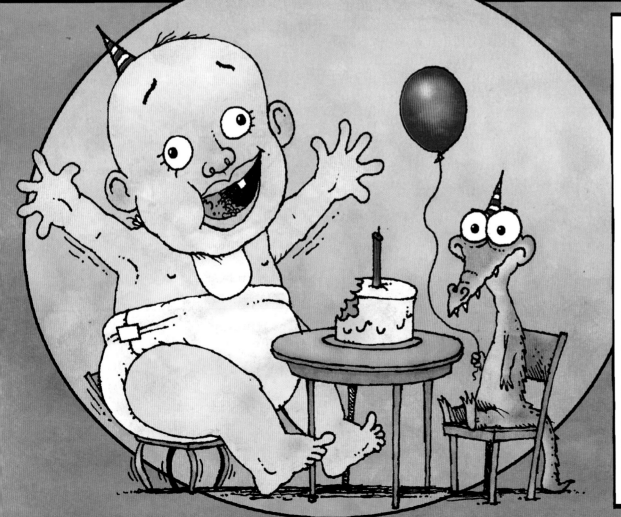

CHILDREN RELY ON THEIR FAMILIES for food, shelter, and protection. Young alligators do too, though not for quite as long. During their first year, they have a rapid growth spurt! American alligators are 8 inches (20 centimeters) at birth, but 24 inches (60 centimeters) within a year. If human babies grew that fast, they'd be 5 feet (1.5 meters) tall on their first birthday. After the first year, alligators grow about a foot annually. By the time they are two years old (and 3 feet [1 meter] long), the alligators have few natural predators. But they've become dangerous in their own right. At this point, their mother or father may send them packing, lest they prey on their younger brothers and sisters.

QUEEN OF THE NILE

THE NILE CROCODILE is among the fiercest of the crocodilians, preying on Cape buffalo, zebras, and even humans. The crocs lie in wait for animals refreshing themselves at the river's edge. When the crocodile lunges, the slippery slope of the riverbank makes escape nearly impossible for the prey. While the Nile crocodile is tough, it isn't invincible—and it sometimes gets a harsh reminder of that. Crocodiles lunging for baby elephants have been trampled by angry elephant mothers and hurled into trees. It's a mistake the crocodiles don't make twice.

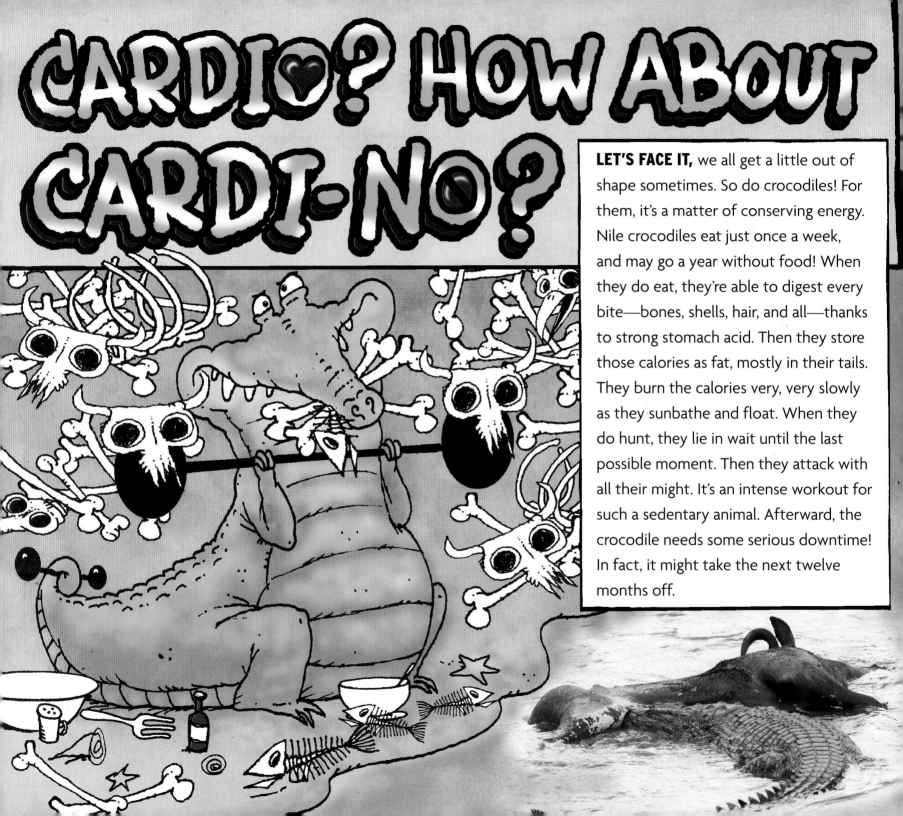

CARDIO? HOW ABOUT CARDI-NO?

LET'S FACE IT, we all get a little out of shape sometimes. So do crocodiles! For them, it's a matter of conserving energy. Nile crocodiles eat just once a week, and may go a year without food! When they do eat, they're able to digest every bite—bones, shells, hair, and all—thanks to strong stomach acid. Then they store those calories as fat, mostly in their tails. They burn the calories very, very slowly as they sunbathe and float. When they do hunt, they lie in wait until the last possible moment. Then they attack with all their might. It's an intense workout for such a sedentary animal. Afterward, the crocodile needs some serious downtime! In fact, it might take the next twelve months off.

Surf's Up! The saltwater crocodile is the largest reptile in the world. Its 3,800-square-mile (10,000-square-kilometer) range—from Southeast Asia to Australia—proves that it's quite the long-distance swimmer. But how can this be? Crocodiles are not known for their endurance. As it turns out, they catch a wave! Saltwater crocodiles wait for a strong current and then hang ten all the way to a new island—traveling as many as 12 miles (19 kilometers) a day. En route, they've been known to prey on large sharks, and have even taken bites out of ships!

WE HUMANS LOVE to play in the sun. It feels good, and vitamin D is good for us! However, we do not need the sun to stay warm. We are *endothermic,* or warm-blooded. That means we maintain approximately the same body temperature whether the air around us is warm or cool. Crocodilians are *ectothermic,* or cold-blooded. The environment determines their body heat. To warm up, they bask in the sun. The problem is, they can't sweat. They open their mouths and let the air cool them. Or they simply take a dip. Aah!

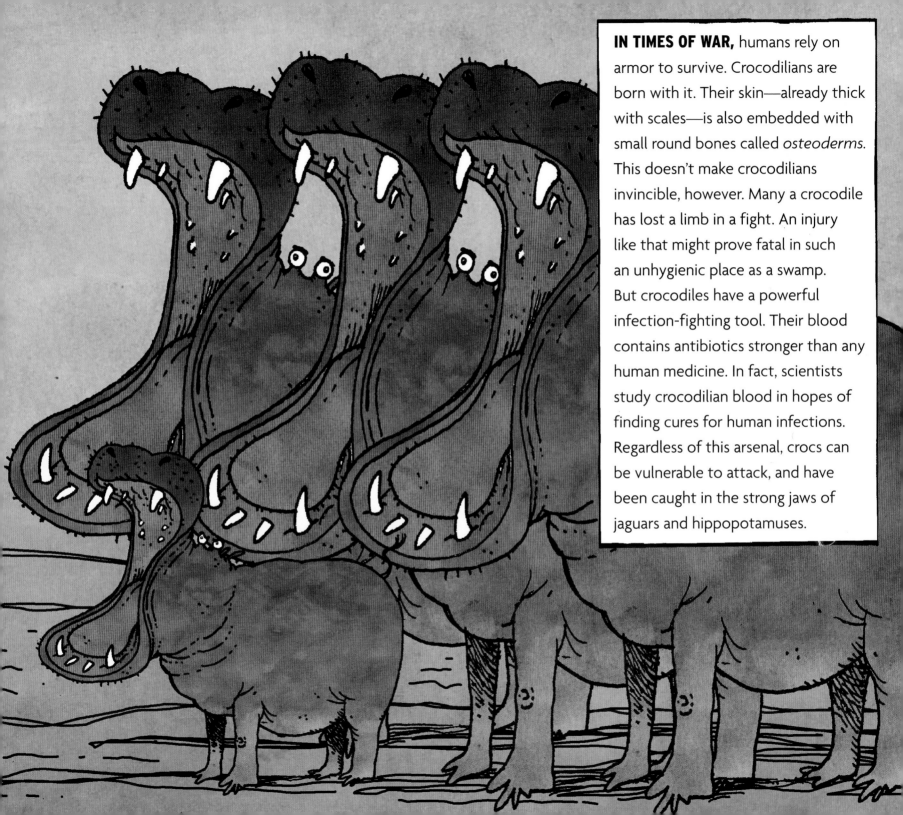

IN TIMES OF WAR, humans rely on armor to survive. Crocodilians are born with it. Their skin—already thick with scales—is also embedded with small round bones called *osteoderms*. This doesn't make crocodilians invincible, however. Many a crocodile has lost a limb in a fight. An injury like that might prove fatal in such an unhygienic place as a swamp. But crocodiles have a powerful infection-fighting tool. Their blood contains antibiotics stronger than any human medicine. In fact, scientists study crocodilian blood in hopes of finding cures for human infections. Regardless of this arsenal, crocs can be vulnerable to attack, and have been caught in the strong jaws of jaguars and hippopotamuses.

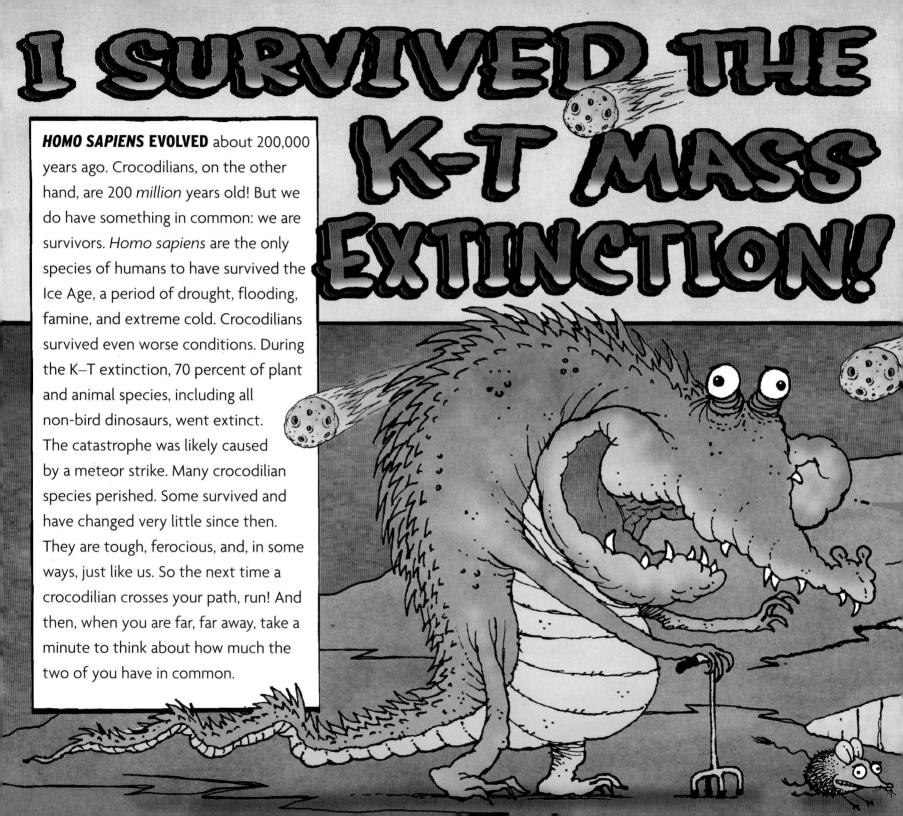

I SURVIVED THE K-T MASS EXTINCTION!

HOMO SAPIENS EVOLVED about 200,000 years ago. Crocodilians, on the other hand, are 200 *million* years old! But we do have something in common: we are survivors. *Homo sapiens* are the only species of humans to have survived the Ice Age, a period of drought, flooding, famine, and extreme cold. Crocodilians survived even worse conditions. During the K–T extinction, 70 percent of plant and animal species, including all non-bird dinosaurs, went extinct. The catastrophe was likely caused by a meteor strike. Many crocodilian species perished. Some survived and have changed very little since then. They are tough, ferocious, and, in some ways, just like us. So the next time a crocodilian crosses your path, run! And then, when you are far, far away, take a minute to think about how much the two of you have in common.

SAY WHAT?

antibiotics medicines or naturally occurring substances that kill harmful microorganisms.

bask to relax in the sun.

bellow to roar, bark, or growl loudly.

calcium a mineral that strengthens bones, teeth, shells, and more.

calorie a unit of energy that can be consumed by eating and burned by exercising.

cold-blooded having a body temperature that depends on the surrounding temperature.

congenial friendly.

crocodilian a large reptile that is either a crocodile, alligator, mugger, caiman, or gharial.

ectothermic being dependent on sources of heat outside one's own body.

endothermic being able to generate heat inside one's own body.

evolve to change gradually as a species because of helpful mutations passed from generation to generation.

extinction the dying off of all animals in a species.

food chain a series of animals, plants, and microorganisms that consume or are consumed by one another.

head slap a crocodilian's action of opening its mouth and shutting it while slapping the lower jaw on the water.

K–T mass extinction the extinction of many plant and animal species, including all non-bird dinosaurs, that marked the end of the Cretaceous—or *Kreidezeit* in German, hence the "K"—Period and the beginning of the Tertiary Period.

litter a group of baby animals born at the same time to the same mother.

marsh a wetland with vegetation that is mostly grass, reeds, or rushes.

osteoderm a small, round bone embedded in the skin.

swamp a wetland with mostly trees or other woody vegetation.

wallow to relax in water or mud.

warm-blooded having a body temperature that does not depend on the surrounding temperature.

wetland an area of land that may include swamps, marshes, or other water-saturated terrain.

yolk the part of an egg that provides nourishment to the embryo inside.

BIBLIOGRAPHY

Alcala, Angel C., and Maria Teresa S. Dy-Liacco. "Habitats." In *Crocodiles and Alligators,* edited by Charles A. Ross. New York: Facts on File, 1989.

Alderton, David. *Crocodiles & Alligators of the World.* New York: Facts On File, 2004

Australian Museum. "The Mesozoic Extinction Event." October 30, 2015. (australianmuseum.net.au/the-mesozoic-extinction-event)

Buffetaut, Eric. "Evolution." In *Crocodiles and Alligators,* edited by Charles A. Ross. New York: Facts on File, 1989.

Campbell, Hamish A., Matthew E. Watts, Scott Sullivan, Mark A. Read, Severine Choukroun, Steve R. Irwin, and Craig E. Franklin. "Estuarine Crocodiles Ride Surface Currents to Facilitate Long-distance Travel." *Journal of Animal Ecology* 79, no. 5 (2010): 955–964. (onlinelibrary.wiley.com/doi/10.1111/j.1365-2656.2010.01709.x/full)

De Roy, Tui. "Night of the Caimans." National Wildlife Federation. February 1, 2003. (www.nwf.org/News-and-Magazines/National-Wildlife/Animals/Archives/2003/Night-of-the-Caimans.aspx)

Lang, Jeffrey W. "Social Behavior." In *Crocodiles and Alligators,* edited by Charles A. Ross. New York: Facts on File, 1989.

Levy, Megan. "Brutus the Monster Crocodile Eats Bull Shark in Northern Territory." *Sydney Morning Herald.* August 6, 2014. (www.smh.com.au/environment/animals/brutus-the-monster-crocodile-eats-bull-shark-in-northern-territory-20140806-100xwq.html)

Lynch, Rene. "5 Ways to Avoid, or Survive, an Alligator Attack." *Los Angeles Times.* July 10, 2012. (articles.latimes.com/2012/jul/10/nation/la-na-nn-alligator-attacks-rare-20120710)

Magnusson, William Ernest, Kent A. Vliet, A. C. Pooley, and Romulus Whitaker. "Reproduction." In *Crocodiles and Alligators,* edited by Charles A. Ross. New York: Facts on File, 1989.

Mazzotti, Frank J. "Structure and Function." In *Crocodiles and Alligators,* edited by Charles A. Ross. New York: Facts on File, 1989.

Naish, Darren. "Crocodiles Attack Elephants." *Scientific American.* February 4, 2013. (blogs.scientificamerican.com/tetrapod-zoology/crocodiles-attack-elephants)

National Park Service. "American Alligator: Species Profile." (www.nps.gov/ever/learn/nature/alligator.htm; accessed March 5, 2017.)

Nova. "Crocodiles!" Transcript. Aired April 28, 1998, on PBS. (www.pbs.org/wgbh/nova/transcripts/2509crocs.html)

Pooley, A. C. "Food and Feeding Habits." In *Crocodiles and Alligators,* edited by Charles A. Ross. New York: Facts on File, 1989.

Pooley, A. C., and Charles A. Ross. "Mortality and Predators." In *Crocodiles and Alligators,* edited by Charles A. Ross. New York: Facts on File, 1989.

Ross, Charles A., and William Ernest Magnusson. "Living Crocodilians." In *Crocodiles and Alligators,* edited by Charles A. Ross. New York: Facts on File, 1989.

University of Florida. "Alligator Holes." (www.flmnh.ufl.edu/southflorida/habitats/freshwater-marshes/alligator-holes; accessed March 5, 2017.)

Villareal, Rene. "*Paleosuchus trigonatus:* Schneider's Smooth-fronted Caiman, Cachirre, Jacaré coroa." Animal Diversity Web. 2003. (animaldiversity.org/accounts/Paleosuchus_trigonatus)

Wurts, William A. "Why Can Some Fish Live in Freshwater, Some in Salt Water, and Some in Both?" Kentucky State University. March 1998. (www2.ca.uky.edu/wkrec/vertebratefishevolution.pdf)

BRIDGET HEOS is the author of more than one hundred nonfiction titles for kids and teens, including *Shell, Beak, Tusk; Stronger Than Steel; It's Getting Hot in Here; I, Fly;* and *What to Expect When You're Expecting Larvae.* She's also the author of the picture books *Mustache Baby* and *Mustache Baby Meets His Match.* Bridget lives in Kansas City with her husband and four children, and you can learn more about her and her books at authorbridgetheos.com.

DAVID CLARK has illustrated numerous picture books, including *Pirate Bob, Fractions in Disguise,* and *The Mine-o-Saur.* He also co-created—and illustrates—the nationally syndicated comic strip *Barney & Clyde.* David lives in Virginia with his family, and you can learn more about his books and his comics at sites.google.com/site/davidclark1988.

Photo Credits: Lloyd Paul Aiello: 9 • Francois Borman: 21 • Thierry Chardes: 6 • Michael Freeman: 11, cover • Roger and Pat de la Harpe: 15, 17, 29, cover • Ken Kiefer: 25 • Leonardo Prest Mercon Rocha: 16, cover • Newan Samaranayake: 4, cover • Devaka Seneviratne: 12 • Stephen and Ann Toon: 26 • Ariadne Van Zanderbergen: 22